The True Grimoire of Demonolatry

ISBN 9798604708316

ALSO BY ARUNDELL OVERMAN
(DIABLITO ORDO AL GHOUL)

Liber Asmodeus

The Al Ghoul Compendium, or the Black Book of the Grey Man

The Sorcery Party:
A Training Manual for the Nagual

Five Hundred Real Dreams:
A Witch's Dream Journal

The Infernal Dictionary:
Devils, Gods, and Spirits of the Dictionnaire Infernal

Spells of the Grimoires

The Illustrated Grand Grimoire

The Lore of Asmoday

The Werewolf in Theory and Practice

Shemhamephorash:
A Study of the 80 Infernal Names Found in the Satanic Bible

The Illustrated Goetia:
Lesser Key of Solomon

Liber Spiritum:
A Witch's Book of Spirits

The Order of the Demon Star

The Diary of a Skinwalker

Contents

The True Grimoire of Demonolatry, or
The Grimorium Verum for Demonolaters
by
Arundell Overman

Introduction

Hello and welcome to *The True Grimoire of Demonolatry*! *The Grimorium Verum*, Latin for *True Grimoire*, is a grimoire said to have been written by Alibeck the Egyptian of Memphis in 1517. In this book we will be using the terms *Grimorium Verum* and *True Grimoire* in equal measure. *The True Grimoire*, like many of the grimoires, claims to have originated with King Solomon. In this edition of *The True Grimoire*, *The Grimorium Verum*, we will be examining the book from the perspective of a Pagan, a Demonolater, and a Satanist.

Definitions

Let us start with a few definitions. *Demonolatry* is the worship of demons. Demons (in the case of the grimoires) are, for the most part, ancient gods who have been assigned to the underworld of hell by the Christian religion. For instance, the demons Astaroth and Beelzebub, two of the chief spirits of *The True Grimoire*, were once the Canaanite goddess Astarte and the god Beelzebub. Over time, due to their "demonization" in the Christian Bible, these ancient deities became demons in the grimoires, as have many other ancient gods and goddesses.

The term *Pagan* is generally applied to those who worship pre-Christian gods. The god Beelzebub, who was mentioned in the Bible (first in the Old Testament as the "god of Ekron," and then in the New Testament as "the Prince of Demons"), could be said by one definition to be a Pagan god, and by another definition to be a Christian demon. In this case, what is the difference between Pagan god and Demon?

The original book, *The Grimorium Verum* or *True Grimoire*, written around 1517, is set within the perspective of all the grimoires, that of a heretical Christian of sorts. Yet one must remember that the penalty for getting caught invoking any of the demons listed in any of the grimoires was death by hanging or by being burned at the stake. So anyone who would be brave enough to carry out the instructions of the grimoires was certainly practicing witchcraft and heresy—damnable arts—even if reciting bible verses while doing it.

The Grimoires

Etymologically, the word *grimoire* translates to "instruction manual" and refers to hundreds of distinct books written and printed during the development of the European Gutenberg printing press in the 1400s, all the way through the early 1800s. These "cookbooks" contained spells and recipes for various things such as winning the love of a person, for safety, health, controlling the weather, making talismans, finding lost objects or hidden treasure, timetables for planting crops, invoking good angels, and in the case of some of the darker grimoires, invoking the devil and various demons. It is precisely these darker, more "sinister" grimoires (especially the "True Grimoire" or *Grimorium Verum*), which concern us in the study of this book.

Along with *The Lesser Key of Solomon: The Goetia*, *The Grand Grimoire*, and *The Grimoire of Honorius*, *The Grimorium Verum* is one of the most important of the grimoires or "instruction manuals" containing the names and offices of demons and how to conjure them to visible appearance to do the will of the operator. All of these books have some sort of Christian or Jewish framework, different for each one, and a method of conjuration. Let's take a brief look at each of these other books to better understand *The True Grimoire,* or *Grimorium Verum.*

The Lesser Key of Solomon: Goetia

The Lesser Key of Solomon is perhaps the most famous of the grimoires. It has a catalog of 72 demons that are well-described as to their appearance, and each one is linked to a sigil. Aside from some missing parts in the descriptions of the "four kings" that rule over all the other spirits, the method of invoking the spirits is also workable and comparatively easy to follow.

It was *The Lesser Key* that was my introduction to the grimoires and demonology. When I was 19 or 20 years old (due to hearing about *The Lesser Key* through another book, *Modern Magic*) I ordered a copy of it in the mail. When the book arrived at my house, before I even had a chance to read it, Asmoday came out of the book—just like the proverbial genii from a lamp—and began speaking to me! This permanently changed my life and set me on a lifelong study of the grimoires and the demons. [*This story, and all the legends and lore of the mighty demon Asmoday, are recounted in great detail in my book* The Lore of Asmoday.]

Without exaggeration I can say that due to meeting the demon Asmoday and having an incredibly strong desire to understand who he was and where he came from, I must have read *The Lesser Key of Solomon* 100 times. I made a magic circle drawn on the back of a carpet scrap, and then created each of the 20 or so tools described in the book, such as a magic robe, "hexagram of Solomon" talismans of the spirits to be worn when invoking, a "triangle of the art" to call the spirits into a "brass vessel," and so forth. Eventually

I would create three different sets of these tools—getting better and better each time—and I would estimate that I performed well over 100 evocations with all of the equipment used in the traditional system described in the book.

In *The Lesser Key*, the magician stands within the magic circle and threatens and binds the demon to appear in the triangle by using the "holy names of God," the angels, and various Bible characters. The demons are viewed as unholy and evil spirits ranked under Satan (the Christian devil), who all live in hell (the Christian underworld). The attitudes shown towards these spirits are of both awe and fear, as well as respect, because it was well-known that these beings were strong and mighty kings and rulers within their own realms and worlds.

For my part, when I began practicing *The Goetia*, it was right before the development of the internet, and I knew of no other person on earth who knew anything about it. The book itself was all I had. I only knew of one way to call the spirits, and that was the way described in the book, as harsh and old fashioned as it was.

Eventually I met another magician in my city who was working with *The Grand Grimoire*, and *The Grimorium Verum*, which is also called the "True Grimoire." After starting to study these books and comparing them to *The Lesser Key*, I noticed that they featured many spirits shared in common throughout the books, such as Bael who was in *The Goetia* and *Grand Grimoire*, but there were also many spirits which were in some but not all of the grimoires. For instance, the demon Pruflas is mentioned in *The Grand Grimoire*, but is not found in *The Lesser Key of Solomon*, or *The Grimorium Verum*. Astaroth, however, is the only spirit shared by all these books.

Each grimoire had its own "operating system": a distinct set of tools such as a wand, a magic circle, and set of conjurations. The

operating system of each of these grimoires shared certain similar-
ities, such as a wand made of hazel wood to be used by the magician (mentioned in *The Lesser Key* and *The Grand Grimoire*), but in
The Grand, the wand is described as having a forked tip, and no
such instructions are mentioned in *The Lesser Key*. The hazel wand
is mentioned in conjunction with the spirit Beleth, in *The Lesser Key*.

Therefore, because I had already built an operating system
designed from the instructions of *The Lesser Key*, if I wanted to
contact a spirit found in one of the other books—such as Lucifuge
Rofocale or Pruflas—I had two choices: I could start over and build
a full set of tools from *The Grand Grimoire*, or I could attempt to
use my already created set of tools and operating system from *The
Lesser Key* to conjure a spirit not found in the book.

Because I was very traditional at first, I created a full operating system based on *The Grand Grimoire*. By the time I created it,
however, I had also begun experimenting with using my operating
system from *The Lesser Key* to call spirits not found in the book and
discovered that it worked just as effectively.

Recently in my practice, under the instruction of Asmoday, I
created a modified system with a circle and triangle that does not
invoke the Christian god nor angels. My system modifies the conjurations to be pro-demonolatry, seeing the demons as my gods,
friends, and allies. With this system I can conjure any demon or
Pagan god, goddess, or spirit, from *any* pantheon. The power of this
system relies on the personal will of the magician, the Kundalini
energy, the infinite force of the universe known as the "Bornless
One," and any spirit or deity with whom the magician has made
alliances. [*Full instructions on this system can be found in* The Al Ghoul
Compendium *written under my pen name* Diablito Ordo Al Ghoul].

The Grand Grimoire

The Grand Grimoire uses a circle made from the skin of a sacrificed goat, no sword, a hazel wood wand with a forked tip, and its own unique set of conjurations. It has 27 spirits and its upper hierarchy of nine spirits is identical to *The True Grimoire* with the exception that Lucifuge Rofocale is called Tarchimache in the original *Grimorium Verum*. We will use the name Lucifuge Rofocale here as it is the more commonly used name and seems to carry more power as well.

For those who do not have the ability to sacrifice a goat nor prepare a magic circle with strips of its skin, *The Grand Grimoire* offers a second, more stripped-down, version of the ritual: The hazel wand, a circle scratched on the ground with a bloodstone, and a pact with a demon, are all that is needed to carry out this work.

The Grand Grimoire, The True Grimoire, The Lesser Key of Solomon, and *The Grimoire of Honorius,* along with all the other grimoires I have ever studied, contain sets of instructions devoted to the preparation of the operator. These involve periods of fasting, or moderation of diet, and sexual abstinence. While many people tend to see these only as Christian-like moralizing, magicians who have followed the given instructions to the letter have reported great benefits from doing so. These kinds of sacrifices are mentioned dozens if not hundreds of times within the grimoires, both in the preparation period before invoking spirits and as essential components of countless spells. [*See my book* Spells of the Grimoires *for many examples of these within grimoire spells.*]

The earliest edition of *The Grand Grimoire* dates back to 1750, and as such was likely written 200 years after *The True Grimoire*. It is possible that *The Grand Grimoire* was created from *The Grimorium Verum* or that, at the very least, they had a common ancestor. It should be noted that there were at one time hundreds of these types of grimoires in circulation and often they borrowed from each other, but the original editions were largely lost, destroyed, or printed in secret. Thus, the history of these books is indeed a very tangled one. Regardless, the *Grand* and the *Verum* are strongly related, and their upper hierarchy of nine spirits is identical.

The Grimoire of Honorius

The Grimoire of Pope Honorius, or *Le Grimoire du Pape Honorius*, is a 17th-18th century grimoire, which claims to have been written by Pope Honorius III (1150-1227). It is unique among the grimoires because it was intended to be used by a priest and the instructions include celebrating a Mass. Many of the spirits included parallel *The True Grimoire*, and its text will be often noted here.

The True Grimoire

All of the grimoires have missing parts or sigils, or include instructions that seem contradictory. This occurs for several reasons. First, during the time in which they were written, owning a grimoire could land you in trouble. Getting caught in the act of using one could get you hanged or burned at the stake, even if the book was "written by King Solomon," "Saint Cyprian," or, "a long dead Pope." Indeed, owning or using these books was a very serious and risky undertaking. The grimoires were mostly handwritten or copied in secret from one manuscript to another. This frequently led to errors, changes in the names of demons, diagrams, sigils, and pages becoming lost, and so forth.

As was the case with many grimoires, they were printed on clandestine printing presses that did not print the locations of their publication nor their correct publication dates. There were hundreds—if not thousands—of these types of books printed over time, yet their content was almost entirely correlated, like branches of the same tree. Moreover, most of the grimoires (if not all) had an abundance of authors, even if they were only attributed to a few historical or Biblical figures. For instance, King Solomon most certainly did *not* write any of these books. However, he is primarily attributed to them.

The Bible posits that, in his later years, King Solomon "followed not completely after his God Yahweh." Though he is famous, in part, for building the first stationary temple to the Hebrew god, it is recorded in the Bible that he also built a temple for the Pagan goddess Astarte as well as the god Chemosh. The Bible blames this heresy on the influence of his foreign wives. It is believed that this temple of Chemosh existed for 400 years until finally being torn down during the reform of Josiah.

The reputation of Solomon as a magician, who had bound "unruly demons" and "Pagan gods" to assist him in the building of the temple of Yahweh, was well established by 100 A.D., as is described in the "Testament of Solomon," which dates to this time period. In this testament, Solomon, through the power of his magic ring (echoes of which we see in *The Lesser Key*), binds such powerful demons as Belzebuth and Asmodeus, forcing them to reveal to him many secrets and to carry out construction on the temple.

The Testament of Solomon was an early model for the development of many later grimoires such as *The Lesser Key*, *The True Grimoire*, etc. Over time the lists of spirits changed from book to book as spirits were added into the mix, or (in some cases) were lost. Sometimes, names of spirits would get changed due to the material being translated in a country with a different language. Once again, all of the grimoires created after the invention of the Gutenberg press up until the 1800s were developed during a time when getting caught using one could land you in jail or tied to a stake, so there was a great deal of secrecy involved in the writing process and distribution of these books.

The True Grimoire, or *Grimorium Verum* has suffered a few wounds during the journey from its original composition in 1517 to the current year (2020). There are a few missing sigils that have been misplaced from edition to edition. Anyone who would approach the book with a mind to attempt its processes will have to do a bit of reconstruction to make it workable. For my part, I will attempt to first present the historical text of the book as it was originally written and make clear notes of any instances in which I have filled in the gaps and the reasoning as to why.

Three Ways to Use This Book

The list of spirits in *The True Grimoire* is complicated and written in a very difficult-to-follow manner as compared to *The Grand Grimoire* or *The Lesser Key of Solomon*. The purpose of the spirit list at the end of this book is to make the spirits more accessible, and is numbered from 1-44, much like the 1-72 list in *The Lesser Key*. All of the sigils of the spirits, along with their powers and descriptions, and when possible their images, are listed in order at the end of this book.

You can use *The Grimorium Verum, The True Grimoire*, in one of several ways. First, you can simply attempt to follow the original instructions exactly as they are described in the original text. Many hundreds of people, perhaps even thousands of people, have attempted this. I did it for 20 years with *The Lesser Key*. Eventually I arrived at a moment in which I decided that I simply did not wish to incorporate anything "Christian" into my practice, even if it was used in the process of invoking the demons. So, I simply stopped using anything that was Christian, like Psalms, or names of angels.

This leads us to the second approach in which one uses the basic tools of the system, such as wands, tools, magic circles, and even conjurations, but simply omits any references to the Christian god, Jesus, saints, or the angels. This approach takes careful study and a creative will to modify the original system to make it one's own.

The third approach is taken by those who already have a system or set of methods for invoking spirits. For them, the spirit list of 44 spirits at the end of this book will be the most valuable part of the book. These 44 are the mighty demons of *The True Grimoire, The Grimorium Verum*.

1.   Work the book exactly as it is described, including the use of Christian psalms, prayers, and angels.

2.   Work with the book in a slightly modified manner, using its tools, such as wands, knives, "virgin" parchment, and invocations, but excluding or modifying all Christian parts, such as Psalms, and so forth; this is the demonolatry or "devil worshipper" approach. One might also say it is a Pagan way. The spirits are demons and old gods. As a Pagan, a Satanist,

or a Demonolater, you would want to make sure to replace any Christian names on magical circles or tools with demon names or sigils. You would also need to modify any prayers or Psalms to include demons and the devil rather than angels or the Christian god or saints. You might also choose to include invoking Left Hand Path saints such as Anton Lavey, Aleister Crowley, or Marie Laveau.

3.   Incorporate the spirits from the list within *The True Grimoire* into your already established "operating system" of magic, and directly invoke them by means of their names, sigils, and when possible, their images. Even drawing the sigils by hand while reading the names and powers of the spirits will draw them to you to some degree.

If you don't already have an operating system, meaning "a system of tools, conjurations, and formulas" to invoke spirits or practice witchcraft, Paganism, or Satanism, I would suggest option two. Take the time to carefully read the text of *The True Grimoire*, and then strike out on your own, trying to contact the spirits and create an "operating system" of tools and a notebook full of conjurations with which to summon the spirits. The 44 spirits of *The Grimorium Verum* form, in a very real sense, a pantheon of gods. The demon Scirlin is the "messenger of the gods," or, the one who connects you to the others. He can help summon any of these gods for you—and perhaps many—if you have a good relationship with him.

In conjunction with your demonic magical practice, I also highly recommend a study of some form of yoga. All forms of yoga awaken a latent force within the body known as *Kundalini* within the body, and it makes your western style of magic, such as that of the grimoires, much more powerful.

To truly become a witch takes time and effort, and it takes time to build a relationship with the spirits as well. Eventually (and if you are properly prepared), they will come to know you quite profoundly and will begin to appear quickly, sometimes even right at the moment you begin the ritual of evocation.

Making Contact With the Spirits

The simplest way to contact the spirits is simply to read their 44 names, given at the end of the book, in a loud and clear voice, with the intent to call upon them. Start from the beginning and read the names aloud and see if you feel anything enter the room with you. You may be very surprised that you feel, see, or hear something when you least expect it. This is a key to magic; you will often feel or see these creatures when you least expect it, and that is one way you know they were not created by your own mind. When you truly get a strong contact with one of these beings, it will be beyond what you have ever expected, both in strength and in magnificence.

Another simple way to contact spirits is to draw their sigil on a candle, and as you light the candle say, "I light this candle in the name and to the honor of Lucifer." (state your petition or goal) "Hail Lucifer!" Or, "Hail Bechard!" or whatever spirit you are invoking during that magical operation. This is a simple, direct way of invoking spirits. The candle itself functions as an offering to the spirit. The words of the conjuration serve to draw it to you, and the sigil of the spirit acts as a key to connecting with it. With this method there is no magic circle, but it might be said that the room you are working in takes on the properties of a temple, no matter how simple your ritual is.

The first thing that you will probably experience is a change in the atmosphere of the room. The air may feel heavier, or lighter, or more electrified. Objects may seem to glow, and time may also seem to slow down or stop. Often the arrival of the spirits will produce an electrical feeling in your aura, i.e., your energy body. This can and does stimulate the chakras, or centers of energy. As the energy rises, various levels of consciousness (or awareness of self, other beings, or dimensions) also awaken.

Once you make contact, depending on various factors such as how often you are doing rituals and the size and strength of your own energy field, many different spirits will come to visit you; some just to "check you out" and see who you are becoming, or others if they wish to teach you or make deals with you. Witches are special to the demons because a witch is someone who spirits can communicate with, as they have one foot in this world and one in the next. So, when you start to become something *more than human*—becoming a witch through the process of performing rituals and carrying out the instructions from a book such as this—many different kinds of spirits begin to take notice and will begin to contact you.

Tools such as wands, circles, and even your "notebooks of conjurations," will become *haunted*. Spirits attach their energy to such objects through their love for them and their desire to contact humans. For spirits often desire to contact us, just as we desire to contact them.

Sigils

Almost every demon has a sigil while some have several, varying from book to book, in the old manuscripts in which the spirit is listed. Whenever I could, I took the time to list the variations in such instances where a spirit has more than one sigil; you may find that one works better for you than another. A few of the spirits do not have sigils, or perhaps the originals were lost over time. In those cases, I channeled a sigil for each of those spirits and carefully noted when a sigil is from the old grimoire or when I filled in the blanks.

I encourage you to experiment with drawing the original sigils as well as trying to channel new ones from the spirits. During your work, the process of drawing sigils already in existence, as well as creating new ones, is a very magical experience. Having a connection with the spirit will often help you to draw the sigil until you get it just right. You will know you got it right (and when there is power within it) when it *feels* right, because it will often "sparkle" or otherwise bend and move before you upon your gaze.

The Magic Circle

Although *The True Grimoire* mentions a magic circle to be used, it does not describe its specific shape nor instructions for creating it. It does, however, provide a hexagram to be drawn at the corners, or compass points. This could be drawn on the ground, or carpet, or on small disks placed outside of the circle. The hexagram can also be modified to be the "unicursal" form, i.e., a six-pointed star drawn with one continuous line, often used by

Crowley. In *The Lesser Key*, this hexagram is to be made on calf skin and worn at the waist just like an apron. It is shown to the spirits upon arrival in an attempt to make them obedient to the will of the operator.

It is also possible due to the wording of the text that the main seals of Lucifer, Belzebuth, and Astaroth given in *The Grimorium Verum* are to be used as the magic circle itself; a different one used for each of the three spirits. A similar interpretation is taught in *The Grimoire of Honorius*, in which specific circles are created for each of the seven spirits assigned to the days of the week. Regardless of what the original method was, it has been lost.

The magician who wishes to carry out the work will have to choose a form of magic circle. One suggestion that has been proposed is the design from *The Grand Grimoire*, as the books are very similar and contain the same upper hierarchy of spirits. The circle shown here is included in *The Grand Grimoire*. The basic design calls for a triangle within a circle, and the spirit should appear anywhere outside the circle to answer your demands. This contrasts with the magic circle given in *The Lesser Key of Solomon*, where the spirit is directed to appear in a triangle drawn outside the circle.

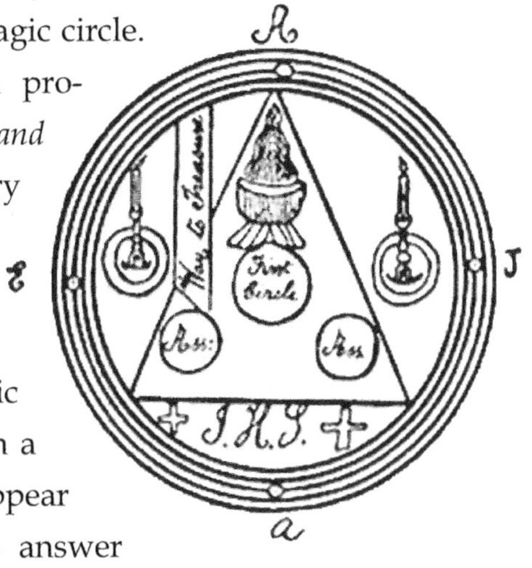

Having worked with *The Lesser Key* in the traditional manner for many years—and having the spirit usually manifest inside the triangle—it was a strange experience for me to first experiment with the magic circle from *The Grand Grimoire*. When the spirit arrived, it waved and danced all around the edges of the magic circle and was not fixed to a specific location in the triangle as I was accustomed to seeing. This was not really a problem; just a different experience for me.

Another form of the magic circle that can be used for working with *The True Grimoire* is the one given in the book of Honorius. It should be remembered that in this introductory essay to *The True Grimoire* we are focusing mainly on *The Lesser Key of Solomon*, *The Grand Grimoire*, and *The Grimoire of Honorius* because they are well known, available, and they relate most closely to that of our present study, *The True Grimoire*, or *The Grimorium Verum*. However, there are dozens, if not hundreds, of examples of magic circles in the various known grimoires that have survived to the present day.

But why use a magic circle at all? If one is going to approach the operation from the perspective of a Demonolater, Pagan, or Satanist (all of whom worship these creatures, these ancient gods), why use a circle to protect yourself from them? The answer is that you *do not* have to use a magical circle at all to invoke demons. Often times demons will appear to you when you are not standing in a magic circle. Even if you previously used a magic circle to invoke them and they subsequently went away, they may suddenly appear to you when you are far from your magic circle, even if in a public place surrounded by throngs of people. Though in my experience this has been rare.

The old magicians who wrote the grimoires and left us these names and sigils of spirits took great care to protect themselves from the spirits they were invoking. Astaroth, one of the three great ruling spirits of *The True Grimoire*, is described in other books as having many different forms; one in which he has poisonous breath that could damage the magician unless they hold the magic ring next to their face. Several other spirits in *The Lesser Key of Solomon* are also mentioned in this regard, such as Amaymon.

Where does this leave us? The truth lies somewhere between "all demons are my friends," and "all demons are out to get me and steal my soul." Demons are independent spirits, roaming the universe and acting out their own free will. Sometimes their free will may be in alignment with your own will; sometimes it may not. The personalities of spirits are as varied as the personalities of the people on Earth. Some are kind and loving, while some are full of greed and malice. Every kind of spirit you can possibly imagine is out there, as are many more which you can't have even imagined of yet.

Using the circle, when properly made, is like piloting a spaceship through other dimensions. During the heat and energy of true invocation of these mighty and ancient beings (with properly prepared tools and a properly prepared operator), there are moments in which it seems time and space are "bent," and you are not sure if the spirit is coming to you, or if you are flying through space toward it or its plane of location.

The circle can provide a strong energetic barrier around your energy field in case you come across a spirit that does wish to attack you. However, it is not just used for protection. Its shape causes it to be a place in which your own personal energy is contained and, therefore, concentrated. The circle is a symbol of *you*: your inner world, your energy sphere, and your aura.

If you have frequently met a spirit whom you have invited into your circle, it is also possible to invite it to enter your body. Most likely, you won't want to do that with all spirits, though. For the most part, it is best to keep the spirits outside of your body and speak to them as friends and allies.

If you have practiced magic for any length of time, you will come across a spirit that you do not like, or, for whatever reason, does not like you. In the latter case, you will be forced to defend yourself or attempt to banish the spirit from around you or a place. This is called *exorcism*. Exorcism can take many forms, even if as simply as burning sage and placing stones in the corners of a room.

Once again, you don't necessarily have to use a circle to practice magic; it is only a tool. It can, however, be a very useful tool even in the sense that the physical circle, when drawn on the ground, acts as a sort of talisman. The circle itself, by way of its design and the words and symbols written upon it, helps to attract the spirits to you. I usually create my magic circles on the back of large squares of carpet. I find that the process of making the magic circle is, well, magical, and that the circle becomes a work of art and of beauty. Often, when I was at peak points in my practice with *The Lesser Key of Solomon*, simply unrolling the carpet and exposing the circle changed the atmosphere in the room and brought in spirits. Whether you use a circle or a "temple" during your rituals, you will feel the electrical or energetic currents in the room change when the ritual is in progress.

While I worked with *The Lesser Key* and *The Grand Grimoire* in the traditional manner, I was never drawn to *The Grimoire of Honorius*. The Catholic nature of its operating system was not something that I ever connected with, having been raised in a protestant branch of Christianity. At this point in my practice I have totally rejected all forms of Christianity, even within the practice of magic, such as using Psalms, the invocation of angels or especially Jesus. So, there is no way I would use the magic circle from Honorius the way it is originally drawn. I do find it to be very interesting, however, that it has the main portion of the circle, in which the magician stands, and then outside of this (within the half circle) the "Spiritus Locus," or the location of the spirit. This is, in a way, very similar to the placement of the triangle outside of the circle shown in *The Lesser Key of Solomon.*

The magic circle from *The Grimoire of Honorius* is shown below, followed by the magic circle from *The Lesser Key of Solomon.*

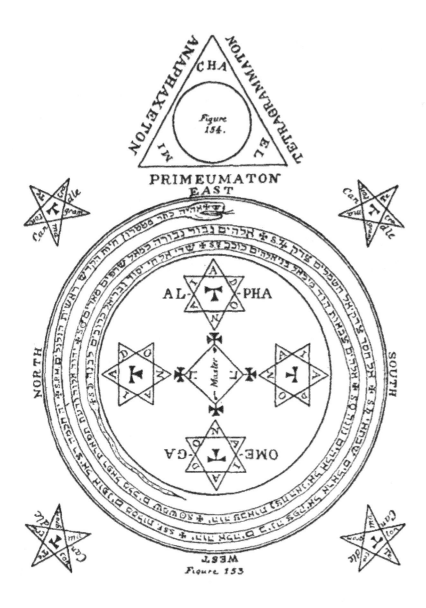

If you choose to work *The True Grimoire* in its traditional manner—Psalms, angels, and all—you will experience great power; of that there is no doubt. You can use any of the three magic circles shown here as your base of operations. Eventually, you will probably come to find, as I did, that you "like" the spirits, you are in awe of them, and you see them as your friends and allies.

If you decide to modify the traditional systems (as I and many others have done), simply follow their instructions to the best of your ability, leaving out the Psalms or Christian parts of the grimoire, or substituting more Satanic or Pagan-themed material.

The Path Less Traveled

Magic will change you; of this there is no doubt. It will put you in contact with forces and knowledge that are outside of what is commonly accepted by society as "normal." You will also, depending on your level of practice, be surrounded by spirits that are from dimensions and planes that most humans are not aware of. These beings will be around, and sometimes *in*, your aura.

Even though "normal" people will not usually be able to directly see these spirits that you have summoned, they will often feel them to some degree. This will make these people uncomfortable around you, or perhaps be drawn to you, while not knowing why. They might only get "weird feelings" around you. This can have both positive and negative effects in your life.

In practice, I recommend that you keep the magical side of your life hidden as much as possible. This way, you don't have to deal with fear or resistance from people who don't resonate with your magic.

Your practice is *completely* up to you. There is nobody in Satanism, Paganism, or Demonolatry who is going to tell you that you are practicing incorrect dogma. Witchcraft—though often practiced in groups or with magical partners—is an individual path; the path less traveled. In this path, *you alone* must stand before the gods. There is no priest or intermediary who will do it for you. In the end, *you alone* must face the great unholy goat, Baphomet, the Lord of the Sabbath of the witches; and it is he who is the face and form of infinity.

Grimorium Verum
or
The True Grimoire

Alibeck the Egyptian, 1517

INTRODUCTION

In the first part is contained various dispositions of characters, by which powers the spirits or, rather, the devils are invoked, to make them come when you will, each according to his power, and to bring whatever is asked: and that without any discomfort, providing also that they are content on their part; for this sort of creature does not give anything for nothing. In the first part is taught the means of calling forth the Elemental Spirits of the Air, Earth, Sea or of the Infernus, according to their affinities.

In the second part are expressed the secrets, both Natural and Supernatural which operate by the power of the Daemons. You will find the manner to make use of them, and all without deceit.

In the third part is the Key to the Work, with the manner of using it. But, before starting this, it will be necessary to be instructed in the following: There are three powers, which are Lucifer, Beelzebuth and Astaroth. You must engrave their Characters in the correct manner and at the appropriate hours. Believe me, all this is of consequence, nothing is to be forgotten.

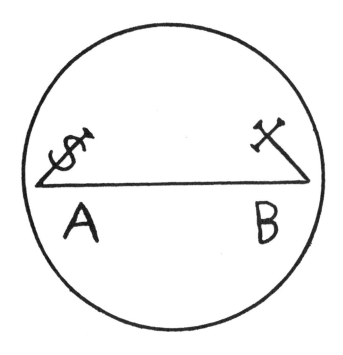

The First Book

CONCERNING THE CHARACTERS OF THE DAEMONS

You must carry the aforesaid character with you. If you are male, in the right pocket, and it is to be written in your own blood, or that of a sea-turtle. You put at the two half-circles the first letter of your name and surname. And if you wish more, you may draw the character on an emerald or ruby, for they have a sympathy for the spirits, especially those of the Sun, who are the most knowledgeable, and are better than the others. If you are a female, carry the character on the left side, between the breasts,

like a Reliquary; and always observing, as much as the other sex, to write or have engraved the character on the day and in the hour of Mars. Obey the spirits in this, that they may obey thee.

The spirits who are powerful and exalted, serve only their confidants and intimate friends, by the pact made or to be made according to certain characters at the will of Singambuth or of his Secretary. Aabidandes, of whom we will give you information, is the perfect acquaintance to call, conjure and constrain, as you will see in the Key, where you will be given a method of making a pact with the spirits.

OF THE NATURE OF PACTS

There are only two kinds of pact, the tacit and the apparent [or explicit]. You will know the one from the other, if you read this little book. Know, however, that there are many kinds of spirits, some attractive and others not attractive.

It is when you make a pact with a spirit and have to give the spirit something which belongs to you, that you have to be on your guard.

THE KINDS OF SPIRITS

Regarding spirits, there are the superior and the inferior. Names of the superiors are: Lucifer, Beelzebuth, Astaroth. The inferiors of Lucifer are in Europe and Asia and obey him. Beelzebuth lives in Africa, and Astaroth inhabits America.

Of these, each of them has two who order their subjects all that which the Emperor has resolved to do in all the world, and vice-versa.

THE VISIBLE APPEARANCE OF SPIRITS

Spirits do not always appear in the same shape. This is because they are not themselves of matter or form, and have to find a body to appear in, and one suitable to their intended manifestation and appearance.

Lucifer appears in the form and figure of a fair boy. When angry, he seems red. There is nothing monstrous about him.

Beelzebuth appears sometimes in monstrous forms, sometimes like a giant cow, at times like a he-goat, with a long tail. When angry, he vomits fire.

Astaroth appears black, in human shape.

Here are characters of Lucifer: [*given at the end of the book*]

The following are those of Beelzebuth and Astaroth: [*given at the end of the book*]

TO INVOKE THE SPIRITS

It is only necessary, when you desire to invoke them, to call them by their characters, which they themselves have given. And when you wish to invoke them, call them to serve you, in the manner taught in the Third Part.

DESCENDING TO THE INFERIORS

Lucifer has two demons under him: Satanackia and Agalierap. Those of Beelzebuth are Tarchimache (Lucifuge Rofocale) and Fleruty. The characters of Satanackia and Fleruty are: [*given at the end of the book*]

The two inferiors of Astaroth are Sagatana and Nesbiros, and their characters are: [*given at the end of the book*].

There are yet other daemons, apart from these, who are under Duke Syrach. There are eighteen of these, and their names are:

I. Clauneck II. Musisin III. Bechaud IV. Frimost V. Klepoth VI. Khil VII. Mersilde VIII. Clisthert IX. Sirchade X. Segal XI. Hicpacth XII. Humots XIII. Frucissiere XIV. Guland XV. Surgat XVI. Morail XVII. Frutimiere XVIII. Huictiigaras

These are the characters of fifteen inferior spirits: [*given at the end of the book*]

The Second Book

AGLA * ADONAY * JEHOVA

There are other daemons, but as they have no power, we shall not speak of them. The powers of the eighteen above-mentioned ones are these:

CLAUNECK has power over riches, can cause treasures to be found. He can give great riches to he who makes a pact with him, for he is much loved by Lucifer. It is he who causes money to be brought.

MUSISIN has power over great lords, teaches all that happens in the Republics, and the affairs of the Allies.

FRIMOST has power over women and girls and will help you to obtain their use.

KLEPOTH makes you see all sorts of dreams and visions.

KHIL makes great earthquakes.

MERSILDE has the power to transport anyone in an instant, anywhere.

CLISTHERT allows you to have day or night, whichever you wish, when you desire either.

SIRCHADE makes you see all sorts of natural and supernatural animals.

HICPACTH will bring you a person in an instant, though he be far away.

HUMOTS can bring you any book you desire.

SEGAL will cause all sorts of prodigies to appear.

FRUCISSIERE revives the dead.

GULAND causes all illnesses.

SURGAT opens every kind of lock.

MORAIL can make anything invisible.

FRUTIMIERE prepares all kinds of feasts for you.

HUICTIIGARAS causes sleep in the case of some, and insomnia in others.

Under Satanachia or Sataniciae are forty-five, or, according to other versions, fifty-four daemons. Four of these, the chiefs, are Sergutthy, Heramael, Trimasael and Sustugriel. The others are of no great consequence.

These spirits are of great advantage, and they work well and speedily, in the case that they are pleased with the operator.

Sergutthy has power over maidens and wives, when things are favorable.

Heramael teaches the art of healing, including the complete knowledge of any illness and its cure, He also makes known the virtues of plants, where they are to be found, when to pluck them, and their making into a complete cure.

Trimasael teaches chemistry and all means of conjuring of the nature of deceit or sleight-of hand. He also teaches the secret of making the Powder of Projection, by means of which the base metals may be turned into gold or silver.

Sustugriel teaches the art of magic. He gives familiar spirits that can be used for all purposes, and he also gives mandragores.

Agalierept and Tarchimache (Lucifuge Rofocale) are the rulers of Elelogap, who in turn governs matters connected with water.

Nebirots rules Hael and Surgulath. The former (Hael) enables anyone to speak in any language he will, and also teaches the means whereby any type of letter may be written. He is also able to teach those things which are most secret and completely hidden.

Sergulath gives every means of speculation. In addition, he instructs as to the methods of breaking the ranks and strategy of opponents. Subject to these are the eight most powerful subordinates:

I. PROCULO, who can cause a person to sleep for forty-eight hours, with the knowledge of the spheres of sleep.

II. HARISTUM, who can cause anyone to pass through fire without being touched by it.

III. BRULEFER, who causes a person to be beloved of women.

IV. PENTAGNONY, who gives the two benefits of attaining invisibility and the love of great lords.

V. AGLASIS, who can carry anyone or anything anywhere in the world.

VI. SIDRAGOSAM, causes any girl to dance in the nude.

VII. MINOSON, is able to make anyone win at any game.

VIII. BUCON, can cause hate and spiteful jealousy between members of the opposite sexes.

The Third Book

THE INVOCATION

ELOY + TAU + VARAF + PANTHON + HOMNORCUM + ELEMIATH + SERUGEATH + AGLA + ON + TETRAGRAMMATON + CASILY

This Invocation is to be made on virgin parchment, with the characters of the Demon upon it, which causes the intermediary Scirlin to come. For from this depend all the others, and it can constrain them to appear in spite of themselves, as he has the power of Emperor.

ORISON: PREPARATION

Lord God Adonay, who hast made man in Thine own image and resemblance out of nothing! I, poor sinner that I am, beg Thee to bless and sanctify this water, so that it may be healthy for my body and my soul, and that all foolishness should depart from it.

Lord God, all-powerful and ineffable, and who led Thy people out of the land of Egypt and has enabled them to cross the Red Sea with dry feet! Accord me this, that I may be purified by this water of all my sins, so that I may appear innocent before Thee! Amen.

When the operator has thus purified himself, he is to set about the making of the Instruments of the Art.

OF THE MAGICAL KNIFE

It is necessary to have a knife or lancet, of new steel, made on the day and hour of Jupiter with the Moon crescent. If it cannot be made, it may be bought, but this must be done at the time, as above.

Having achieved this, you will say the Orison or Conjuration following, which will serve for the knife and lancet.

CONJURATION OF THE INSTRUMENT

I conjure thee, O form of the Instrument, by the authority of our Father God Almighty, by the virtues of Heaven and by the Stars, by the virtue of the Angels, and by the virtue of the Elements, by the virtues of the stones and herbs, and of snow-storms, winds and thunder: that thou now obtain all the necessary power into thyself for the perfecting of the achievement of those things in which we are at present concerned! And this without deception, untruth, or anything of that nature whatsoever, by God the Creator of the Sun of Angels! Amen.

Then we recite the Seven Psalms, and afterwards the following words:

Dalmaley lamekh cadat pancia velous merroe lamideck caldurech anereton mitraton: Most Pure Angels, be the guardians of these instruments, they are needed for many things.

THE SACRIFICIAL KNIFE

On the day of Mars [Tuesday] at the New Moon, make a knife of new steel which is strong enough to cut the neck of a kid

with one blow, and make a handle of wood on the same day and in the same hour, and with an engraver you engrave on the handle these characters:

Then asperge and fumigate it, and you have prepared an instrument for service when and where you wish.

THE MANNER OF ASPERGING & FUMIGATION

First, there is the Orison which is needful on asperging, and it is thus recited:

In the name of the immortal God, asperge [N] and clean you of all foolishness and all deceit, and you will be whiter than snow. Amen.

Then pour as the aspersion blessed water thereon, saying:

In the name of the Father + and of the Son + and of the Holy + Ghost, Amen.

These aspersions are necessary for every item of equipment; so also, is the fumigation which follows.

To fumigate, it is necessary to have a cruse, in which you place coal newly kindled with a new fire, and let it be well ablaze. On this you place aromatics, and when perfuming the article in question, say the following:

Angels of God be our help, and may our work be accomplished by you. Zalay, Salmay, Dalmay, Angrecton, Ledrion, Amisor, Euchey, Or. Great Angels: And do thou also, O Adonay, come and

give to this a virtue so that this creature may gain a shape, and by this let our work be accomplished. In the name of the Father + and of the Son + and of the Holy + Ghost, Amen.

Then recite the Seven Psalms which come after Judicum tuum Regida and Laudate Dominum omnes gentes.

OF THE VIRGIN PARCHMENT

Virgin parchment can be made in many ways. Generally, it is made of the skin of a goat or a lamb, or other animal, which must be virgin.

After inscribing on the blade AGLA, and having fumigated it, the knife will serve you for all purposes.

Remember that when you make the Sacrifice in order to obtain the virgin parchment from the kid, all the instruments must be on the altar.

You make the baton [or Rod, staff] of the Art from Hazel wood that has never borne and cut it with a single stoke on the day and in the hour of Mercury [Wednesday], at the Crescent Moon. And you engrave it with the needle, the pen or the lancet, in the following characters:

The seal and character of Frimost to be inscribed on the first Rod:

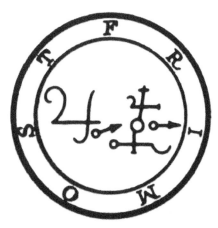

Then you make another baton of Hazel wood, which has never borne, and which is without seed, and cut it in the day and hour of the Sun [Sunday morning at dawn, or Sunday evening at dusk], and on this you engrave these characters:

The seal and character of Klippoth is to be inscribed on the second Rod.

This having been done, you say over your baton the following Orison:

ORISON

Most wise, most powerful Adonay, deign to bless, sanctify and conserve this baton so that it may have the necessary virtue, O most holy Adonay, to whom be honor and glory for all time. Amen.

OF THE LANCET

It is necessary to have a new lancet, conjured and prepared like the knife and sickle. Make it in the day and hour of Mercury, at the Crescent Moon. Now follows the method of Making the Sacrifice of the Kid.

Take your goat and place it on a flat surface, so that the throat is uppermost, the better to cut it. Take your knife and cut the throat with a single stroke, while pronouncing the name of the Spirit you wish to invoke.

For example, you say:

I kill you in the name and in the honor of [N]. . .

This is to be well understood and take care that you sever the throat at first, and do not take two strokes, but see that he dies at the first.

Then you skin him with the knife, and at the skinning make this Invocation:

Adonay, Dalmay, Lauday, Tetragrammaton, Anereton, and all you, Holy Angels of God, come and be here, and deign to infuse into this skin the power that it may be correctly conserved, so that all that is written upon it may become perfected.

After the skinning, take well-ground salt, and strew this upon the skin, which has been stretched, and let the salt cover the skin well. Before you use the salt, it must have the following Benediction said over it.

THE BENEDICTION OF THE SALT

I exorcise you, O creature of the Salt, by the God who is living, the God of all Gods, the Lord of all Lords, that all fantasies may leave you, and that you may be suitable for the virgin parchment.

When this is finished, let the skin with the salt upon it remain in the sun for a full day. Then obtain a glazed pottery jar, and write these characters around it with the Pen of the Art:

Get quicklime and slake this with exorcised water and put these in the jar. When it is liquid place it in your goatskin and leave it long enough for the hairs to peel off themselves.

As soon as the hair is in such a condition as to come off with a touch, remove it from the jar and peel the hairs with a knife made from carved Hazel. The knife must have had these words said over it:

O holiest Adonay, put into this wood the power to cleanse this skin, through the holy name Agason, Amen.

The skin, when peeled, may be stretched over a piece of new wood, and stones are to be placed on the skin, so that they hold it down. These are to be stones from a riverbank. Before placing the stones, say the following Orison over them.

THE ORISON OF THE STONES

O Adonay, most puissant and all-powerful Lord, allow that these stones may stretch this skin, and remove from them all wickedness, so that they may possess the required power. Amen.

OF THE ASPERSION OF THE WATER

All water used in these experiments must be asperged, by saying this over it:

Lord God, Father, all-powerful, my refuge and my life, help me, Holy Father, for I love you, God of Abraham, of Isaac, of Jacob, of the Archangels and Prophets, Creator of All. In humility, and, calling upon Thy holy Name, I supplicate that thou wilt agree to bless this water, so that it may sanctify our bodies and our souls, through Thee, most holy Adonay, Everlasting Ruler, Amen.

The skin is allowed to dry after this, and before quitting the spot, say over the parchment:

Je, Agla, Jod, Hoi, He, Emmanuel! Stand guard over this parchment, in order that no spectra may take charge of it!

When the skin is dry it may be removed from its wooden frame, blessed and fumigated, and then it is ready for use.

It is important that this must not be seen by any women, and more especially during certain times of theirs [i.e., during menstruation], otherwise it will lose its power. It must also be known that when you make and use this parchment, you must be clean, pure and chaste.

The operator is to say one Mass of the Nativity then, and all the instruments are to be on the altar.

OF ASPERSION

You take an asperser made with a bunch of mint, marjoram and rosemary which is secured by a thread which has been made by a virgin maiden.

The asperger is made in the day and hour of Mercury when the Moon is at its crescent.

OF THE PERFUMES

These are to be wood of aloes, incense and mace. As for the mace, this is all that you need for the circle, and over the perfumes is to be said the following Orison:

THE ORISON OF THE AROMATIC PERFUMES

Deign, O Lord, to sanctify the creature of this, in order that it may be a remedy for the human race, and that it may be a remedy for our souls and bodies, through the invoking of Thy holy Name! Agree that all creatures which may breathe in the vapor of this may have wealth of their bodies and souls: through the Lord who has fashioned the time eternal! Amen.

OF THE PEN OF THE ART

Take a new quill, and asperge and fumigate this in the same way as the other instruments, and when you are cutting its points, say:

Ababaloy, Samoy, Escavor, Adonay: I have from this quill driven out all illusions, so that it may hold within it with effectiveness the power needed for all those things which are used in the Art: for both the operations and the characters and conjurations. Amen.

OF THE INKHORN

You buy a new Inkhorn on the day and in the hour of Mercury. At this time, also, these characters are [to be] inscribed upon it:

JOD HE VAU HE + METATRON + JOD + KADOS + ELOHIM SABAOTH

Then newly made ink is exorcised with this exorcism before being placed in the horn:

I exorcise you, Creature of this Ink, by the names Anston, Cerreton, Stimulator, Adonay, and by the Name of He who created all by one word, and who can achieve all, so that you shall assist me in my work, and so this work may be accomplished by my desire, and brought to a successful end through the agreement of God, He who rules all things, and through all things, omnipresent and eternal. Amen.

Then the ink is to be blessed with this Blessing:

Lord God, Almighty, ruler over all and forever, thou who dost cause to take place the greatest wonders in Thy creations, deign to grant the grace of Thy holy spirit through this ink. Bless it, and sanctify it, and impart to it a special power, that whatever we may say or do or desire may be accomplished: through Thee, Most Holy Prince, ADONAY. Amen.

THE PREPARATION OF THE OPERATOR

When the implements are ready, the operator must prepare himself. This is first done by this Preparatory Orison:

Lord God, ADONAY, who hast formed man in Thine image, I, the unworthy and sinful, beseech Thee to sanctify this water, to benefit my body and soul, cause me to be cleansed.

As he says this the operator is to wash his face and hands with the water that he is blessing.

NOTE: This water is to be used for washing the hands and feet, and know also and know and know again that it is necessary and most necessary, to abstain three days from sin: and above all mortally, however much the human frailty may be, and especially guard your chastity.

During the three days, study the book and during this time, pray five times during the day and four times each night, with the following form:

Astrachios, Asach, Ascala, Abedumabal, Silat, Anabotas, Jesubilin, Scingin, Geneon, Domol: O Lord my God, Thou who art seated higher than the Heavens, Thou who art seated higher than the Heavens, Thou who seeth even unto the depths, I pray that Thou unto me the things which I have in my mind and that I may be successful in them: through Thee, O Great God, the Eternal and who reigns for ever and ever. Amen. [Shah gives a note of a variation: "Astrocio, Asath, a sacra Bedrimubal, Felut, Anabotos, Serabilem, Sergen, Gemen, Domos: . . ."]

All this having been done correctly, all that remains is to follow your invocations and draw your characters and you do as follows:

In the day and hour of Mars [Tuesday] the Moon being at the crescent, and at the first hour of the day—which is a quarter of an hour before sunrise—you will prepare a piece of virgin parchment, which shall contain all the characters and the invocations of the spirits which you wish to produce.

For example, in the said day and hour, you will attach to the small finger of the hand (which is the finger of Mercury) a thread spun by a virgin girl, and pierce the finger with the lancet of the Art, to get blood from it, with which you form your Scirlin character, as is given at the commencement of this book. Then write your invocation, which is that which follows. (Character of Scirlin shown at the end of the book)

INVOCATION TO SCIRLIN

HELON + TAUL + VARF + PAN + HEON + HOMONOREUM + CLEMIALH + SERUGEATH + AGLA + TETRAGRAMMATON + CASOLY

You must write the first letter of your name where is the letter A [in the sign & character of Scirlin], and that of your surname where is the letter D. The spirit Aglassis, whose character it is, is very potent to render you service, and will cause you to have power over the other spirits.

Make above the Character of the Spirit that you desire to come and burn incense in his honor. Then make the conjuration which is addressed to the spirit that you want to cause to appear and burn incense in his honor.

CONJURATION FOR LUCIFER

Lucifer, Ouyar, Chameron, Aliseon, Mandousin, Premy, Oriet, Naydrus, Esmony, Eparinesont, Estiot, Dumosson, Danochar, Casmiel, Hayras, Fabelleronthou, Sodirno, Peatham, Come, Lucifer, Amen.

CONJURATION FOR BEELZEBUTH

Beelzebuth, Lucifer, Madilon, Solymo, Saroy, Theu, Ameclo, Sagrael, Praredun, Adricanorom, Martino, Timo, Cameron, Phorsy, Metosite, Prumosy, Dumaso, Elivisa, Alphrois, Fubentroty, Come, Beelzebuth, Amen.

CONJURATION FOR ASTAROTH

Astaroth, Ador, Cameso, Valuerituf, Mareso, Lodir, Cadomir, Aluiel, Calniso, Tely, Plorim, Viordy, Cureviorbas, Cameron, Vesturiel, Vulnavij, Benez meus Calmiron, Noard, Nisa Chenibranbo Calevodium, Brazo Tabrasol, Come, Astaroth, Amen.

After having said seven times the conjuration addressed to superior spirits, you will see the spirit at once appear, to do whatever you desire.

DISMISSAL OF THE SPIRIT

When you have written the conjuration on the virgin parchment, and have seen the spirit, being satisfied, you can dismiss him by saying this:

Ite in pace ad loca vestra et pax sit inter vos redituri ad mecum vos invocavero, in nomine Patris + et Filii + et Spiritus Sancti + Amen.

[Go in peace unto your abode and let there be peace between you and I, and be ready to come to me when you are called, in the name of the Father + and the Son + and of the Holy Spirit + Amen]

CONJURATION FOR INFERIOR SPIRITS

O SURMY + DELMUSAN + ATALSLOYM + CHARUSIHOA + MELANY + LIAMINTHO + COLEHON + PARON + MADOIN + MERLOY + BULERATOR + DONMEDO + HONE + PELOYM + IBASIL + MEON + ALYMDRICTELS + PERSON + CRISOLSAY + LEMON SESSLE NIDAR HORIEL PEUNT + HALMON + ASOPHIEL + ILNOSTREON + BANIEL + VERMIAS + SLEVOR + NOELMA + DORSAMOT + LHAVALA + OMOR + FRAMGAM + BELDOR + DRAGIN + Come, N. . .

DISMISSAL OF THE INFERIOR SPIRIT

G o in peace, N., whence you came, peace be with you, and come every time I shall call you, in the name of the Father + and of the Son + and of the Holy Spirit + Amen.

Then you will burn the characters, because they will serve only once.

ANOTHER CONJURATION

I conjure thee, N., by the name of the Great Living God, Sovereign Creator of all things, that thou appear in human form, fair and agreeable, without noise or inconvenience, to answer truthfully in all the interrogations that I shall make. I conjure thee to do this by the power of the Holy and Sacred Names.

ORISON OF THE SALAMANDERS

Immortal, eternal, ineffable and Holy Father of all things, who is carried by the revolving chariot unceasingly, of the worlds which continually revolve: dominator of the Etherian countries where there is raised the throne of Thy power: above which Thy redoubtable eyes see all, and Thy holy ears hear all Thy children whom Thou hast loved since the birth of the centuries: for thy golden and great and eternal majesty shines above the world, the sky and the stars, Thou art elevated above all, O sparkling fire, and Thou illuminatest Thyself by Thy splendor, and there go out from Thy essence untarnishable rays of light which nourish Thy infinite spirit. That infinite spirit produces all things, and makes the mighty treasure which cannot fail, to the creation which surrounds Thee, due to the numberless forms of which she bears, and which Thou hast filled at the start. From this spirit comes also the origin of those most holy kings who are around Thy throne, and who compose Thy court, O Universal Father!

O Unique One, O Father of happy mortals and immortals! Thou hast created in particular the powers which are marvelously like the eternal thought, and from Thy adorable essence. Thou hast established them over the angels, thou hast created a third kind of sovereign in the elements. Our continual exercise is to worship Thy desires. We burn with the desire to possess Thee, O Father, O Mother, the most tender of Mothers! O wonderful example of feelings and tenderness of Mothers! O Son, the flower of all sons! O Form of all forms! Soul, Spirit, Harmony, and Name of all things preserve us, and we shall be blessed. Amen.

OF THE PENTACLE AND THE MANNER OF WORKING

I have put here the form of the Pentacle of Solomon so that you may make the arrangements, they being of great importance.

When you make your circle, before entering therein, it is to be perfumed with musk, amber, aloes wood and incense. And for the perfume which you will need for the invocations, that is incense alone.

It is to be observed that you need to have always a fire during invocations, and when you perfume, this will be in the name of the spirit that you would invoke. When you are placing the perfume on the fire, say all the time:

I burn this, N., in the name and to the honor of N.

It is to be remembered that you must hold the invocation in the left hand, and in the right a rod of elder, and a ladle and a knife are to be at your feet.

When all this is ready, stand inside the circle. If you have companions with you, they are to hold a hand one of the other. When inside, trace the form of the circle with the knife of the Art.

Then pick up the wands, one after the other, reciting the Fiftieth Psalm. When the circle is complete, perfume and sprinkle it with holy water. Characters are to be written at the four corners of the circle. There are generally four pentacles, one at each point of the compass; and the spirit is prohibited specifically from entering into the precincts of the circle.

Then the invocations are to be repeated seven times. When the spirit appears, make him sign the character which you are holding in your hand, which promises that he will come whenever you may call him. Ask for what you think needed, and he will give it to you.

DISMISSAL OF THE SPIRIT

L et him go away in these words:

Ite in pace ad loca vestra et pax sit inter vos redituri ad mecum vos invocavero, in nomine Patris + et Filii + et Spiritus Sancti + Amen.

[Go in peace unto your abode and let there be peace between you and I, and be ready to come to me when you are called, in the name

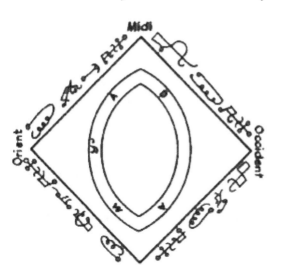

of the Father + and the Son + and of the Holy Spirit + Amen]

This is the character of Scirlin to be drawn on the paper which contains the invocation of the spirit you wish to call.

RARE & SURPRISING MAGICAL SECRETS

The manner of making the Mirror of Solomon, useful for all divinations.

In the name of the Lord, Amen. YE shall see in this mirror anything which you may desire. In the name of the Lord who is blessed, in the name of the Lord, Amen. Firstly, you shall abstain from all actions of the flesh, and also from any sin, whether in word or action, during the period of time laid down herein. Secondly, you must perform acts of good and piety. Thirdly, take a plate of finest steel, burnished and slightly curved, and with the blood of a white pigeon write upon it, at the four corners, these names: JEHOVA, ELOYM, METATRON, ADONAY.

Place the steel in a clean, white cloth. Look for the new Moon, in the first hour after the Sun has set, and when you see it, go to a window, look devoutly towards Heaven, and say:

O Eternal, O King Eternal! God Ineffable! Thou, who hast created all things for the love of men, and by a concealed decision for the wellbeing of man, deign Thou to look on me, N., who am Thy most unfit and unworthy Servant, and look upon this, which is my intention.

Deign to send unto me Thine Angel, Anael upon this same mirror; he does command and order his companions whom Thou hast formed, O Most Powerful Lord, who hast always been, who art, and who shall ever be, so that in Thy name they may work and act with equity, giving me knowledge in everything that I shall seek to know of them.

Now you are to throw down upon the burning embers a perfume.

While you are doing this, say:

In this and with this, that I pour forth before Thy face, O God, my God, Thou who art blessed, Three in One, and in the state of exaltation most sublime, who sits above the Cherubim and Seraphim, who will judge the earth by fire, hear me!

This is to be said three times. When you have done so, breathe three times upon the surface of the mirror, and say:

Come, Anael, come: and let it be thy agreement to be with me willingly: in the name + of the Father, the Most Puissant, in the name + of the Son, Most Wise, in the name + of the Holy Spirit, the Most Living!

Come, Anael, in the terrific name of Jehova! Come, Anael, by the power of the everliving Elohim! Come, thee, by the right arm of the mighty Metatron!

Come to me, N., and order thy subjects so that they may make known to me through their love, joy and peace, the things that are hidden from my eyes.

When you have finished this, raise your eyes toward Heaven and say:

O most powerful Lord, who does cause all things to move in accordance with Thy will, listen to my prayer, and may my intentions be agreeable to Thee! O Lord, if it be Thy will, deign to gaze upon this mirror and sanctify it, that Thy Servant Anael may come thereto with his companions, and be agreeable to me, N., Thy poor and humble servant! O God, blessed and raised above all the spirits of Heaven, Thou who livest and reignest for all time. Amen.

When this is done, make the Sign of the Cross over yourself, and also on the mirror on the first day, and also on the next forty and five days. At the end of this time, the angel Anael will appear to

you, like unto a beautiful child. He will greet you, and will order his companions to obey you.

It does not always require as long as this to cause the angel to appear, however. He may come on the fourteenth day, but this will depend upon the degree of application and fervor of the operator.

When he comes, ask him whatever you may desire, and also beg him to come and do your will whenever you shall call him.

When you want Anael to come again, after the first time, all you have to do is to perfume the mirror, and say these words: Come, Anael, come, and let it be thy agreement --and the rest of this prayer to Anael as we have given you above, until the Amen.

DISMISSING THE SPIRIT

When he has answered your questions, and you are satisfied with him, you must send him away by saying this:

I thank thee, Anael, for having appeared and having fulfilled my requests. Thou mayest therefore depart in peace, and shall return when I call unto thee.

The perfume of Anael is saffron.

DIVINATION BY THE WORD OF URIEL

To succeed in this operation, he who makes the experiment must do all things which are told herein. He is to choose a small room or place which for nine days or more has not been visited by women in an impure state [i.e., during their period].

This place must be well cleaned and consecrated, by means of consecrations and aspersions. In the middle of the room there is to be a table covered with a white cloth. On this is a new glass vial full of spring water, brought shortly before the operation, with three small tapers of virgin wax mixed with human fat; a piece of virgin parchment, and the quill of a raven suitable for writing with; an inkpot of chine full of fresh ink; a small container of metal with materials to make a fire.

You must also find a boy of nine or ten years old, who shall be well behaved and cleanly dressed. He should be near the table.

A large new needle is taken, and one of the three tapers is mounted upon it, six inches behind the glass. The other two tapers should be positioned at the right and left of the glass, and an equal distance away.

While you are doing this, say:

Gabamiah, Adonay, Agla, O Lord of Powers, aid us!

Place the virgin parchment on the right of the glass and the pen and ink on the left. Before starting, close the door and windows.

Now stir the fire, and light the wax tapers. Let the boy be on his knees, looking into the glass vial. He should be bareheaded and his hands joined.

Now the Master orders the boy to stare fixedly into the vial, and speaking softly into his right ear, he says:

THE CONJURATION

URIEL + SERAPH + JOSATA + ABLATI + AGLA + CAILA, I beg and conjure thee by the four words that God spoke with His mouth to His servant Moses: JOSTA + AGLA + CAILA + ABLATI. And by the name of the Nine Heavens in which thou livest, and also by the virginity of this child who is before thee, to

appear at once, and visibly, to reveal that truth which I desire to know. And when this is done, I shall discharge thee in peace and benevolence, in the Name of the Most Holy Adonay.

When this conjuration is finished, ask the child whether he sees anything in the vial. If he answers that he sees an angel or other materialization, the Master of the operation shall say in a friendly tone:

Blessed spirit, welcome. I conjure thee again, in the Name of the Most Holy Adonay, to reveal to me immediately . . . . (Here the operator petitions the spirit for what he will.)

Then say to the spirit:

If, for any reason, thou dost not wish what thou sayest to be heard by others, I conjure thee to write the answer upon this virgin parchment, between this time and the morrow. Otherwise thou mayst reveal it to me in my sleep.

If the spirit answers audibly, you must listen with respect. If he does not speak, after you have repeated the supplication three times, snuff the tapers, and leave the room until the following day. Return the next morning, and you will find the answer written on the virgin parchment, if it has not been revealed to you in the night.

DIVINATION BY THE EGG

The operation of the Egg is to know what will happen to anyone who is present at the experiment.

One takes an egg of a black hen, laid in the daytime, breaks it, and removes the germ.

You must have a large glass, very thin and clear. Fill this with clear water and into it put the egg-germ.

The glass is placed in the Sun at midday in summer, and the Director of the operation will recite the prayers and conjurations of the day.

These prayers and conjurations are such as are found in the Key of Solomon, in which we treat amply of airy spirits.

And with the index finger, agitate the water, to make the germ turn. Leave it to rest a moment, and then look at it through the glass, not touching it. Then you will see the answer, and it should be tried on a working-day, because these are spirits that will come during the times of ordinary occupations.

If one wishes to see if a boy or a girl is a virgin, the germ will fall to the bottom; and if he (or she) is not, it will be as usual.

TO SEE SPIRITS OF THE AIR

Take the brain of a cock, the powder from the grave of a dead man (which touches the coffin), walnut oil and virgin wax. Make all [this] into a mixture, wrapped in virgin parchment, on which is written the words:

GOMERT KAILOETH, with the character of Khil.

Burn it all, and you will see prodigious things. But this experiment should be done only by those who fear nothing.

TO MAKE 3 GIRLS OR 3 GENTLEMEN APPEAR IN YOUR ROOM, AFTER SUPPER

It is necessary to be three days chaste, and you will be elevated.

I. Preparation. On the fourth day, as soon as it is morning, clean and prepare your room, as soon as you have dressed. You must be fasting at this time. Make sure that your room will not be disturbed for the whole of the ensuing day. Note that there shall be nothing hanging, neither anything crosswise to anything else, no tapestries or clothes hanging, and no hats or cages of birds, or curtains of the bed, and so on.

Above all, make sure that everything is clean in every way.

II. Ceremony. After you have supped, go secretly to your room, which has been cleansed as already described. Upon the table there is now to be set a white cloth, and three chairs at the table. In front of each place, set a wheaten roll and a glass of clear and fresh water. Now place a chair at the side of the bed, and retire, while saying this:

III. Conjuration. Besticitum consolatio veni ad me vertat Creon, Creon, Creon, cantor laudem omnipotentis et non commentur. Stat superior carta bient laudem omviestra principiem da montem et inimicos meos o prostantis vobis et mihi dantes que passium fieri sincisibus.

The three people, having arrived, will sit by the fire, eating and drinking, and will thank the person who has entertained them. If you are a gentleman, three girls will come; but if you are a lady, three young men will be involved.

Then the three will draw lots as to whom is to stay with you. If the operator is a man, the girl who wins will sit in the chair which

you have placed by the bed, and she will stay and be with you until midnight. At this time, she will leave, with her companions, without having been dismissed.

The two others will stay by the fire, while the first entertains you.

While she is with you, you may ask her any question about any art or science, or upon any subject at all, and she will at once give you a definite reply. You can ask the whereabouts of hidden treasure, and she will tell you where it is, and how and when to remove it. If the treasure is under the guardianship of infernal spirits, she will come herself, with her companions, and defend you against these fiends.

When she leaves, she will give you a ring. If you wear this on your finger, you will be fortunate at gambling. If you place it on the finger of any woman or girl, you will be able at once to obtain your will of her. Note: The window is to be left open. You can do this experiment as often as you please.

TO MAKE A GIRL COME TO YOU, HOWEVER MODEST SHE MAY BE

Experiment of a marvelous power of the superior intelligences.

Watch for the crescent or the waning moon, and when you see it, make sure that you see also a star, between the hours of eleven and midnight. Before beginning the process, do thus:

Take a virgin parchment and write on it the name of the girl whom you desire to come. The shape of the parchment is to be as you see in this figure:

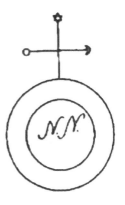

On the other side of the parchment, write MELCHIAEL, BARESCHAS. Then put the parchment on the earth, with the part where the name of the person is written next to the ground. Place your right foot upon the parchment, and your left knee, bent, upon the ground.

Then look to the highest star in the sky, while in this position. In your right hand hold a taper of white wax, sufficiently large to burn for one hour. Then say the following:

THE CONJURATION

I salute thee and conjure thee, O beautiful Moon, O most beautiful Star, O brilliant light which I have in my hand. By the light which I have in my hand. By the air that I breathe within me, by the earth that I am touching: I conjure thee. By the names of the spirit princes living in you. By the ineffable name ON, which created everything! By you, O resplendent angel GABRIEL, with the planet Mercury, Prince, MICHIAEL and MELCHIDAEL.

I conjure you again, by all the Holy Names of God, so that you may send down power to oppress, torture and harass the body and soul and the five senses of N., she whose name is written here, so that she may come unto me. Let her then be tortured, made to suffer. Go, then, at once! Go, MELCHIDAEL, BARESCHES, ZAZEL, FIRIEL, MALCHA, and all those who are with thee! I conjure you by the Great Living God to obey my will, and I, N., promise to satisfy you.

When this conjuration has been said three times, burn the parchment with the taper. On the next day, take the parchment, put it in your left shoe, and let it stay there until the person whom you have

called comes to seek you out. In the conjuration you must say the date that she is to come, and she will not be absent.

TO MAKE ONESELF INVISIBLE

Collect seven black beans. Start the rite on a Wednesday, before sunrise. Then take the head of a dead man and put one of the black beans in his mouth, two in his eyes and two in his ears. Then make upon his head the character of Morail.

When you have done this, bury the head, with the face upwards, and for nine days, before sunrise, water it each morning with excellent brandy. On the eighth day you will find the spirit mentioned, who will say to you: "What wilt thou?"

You will reply: "I am watering my plant." Then the spirit will say: "Give me the bottle, I desire to water it myself." In answer, refuse him this, even though he will ask you again.

Then he will reach out with his hand and will display to you that same figure which you have drawn upon the head. Now you can be sure that it is the right spirit, the spirit of the head. There is a danger that another one might try to trick you, which would have evil consequences—and in that case your operation would not succeed.

Then you may give him the bottle, and he will water the head and leave. On the next day-which is the ninth--when you return, you will find the beans that are germinating. Take them and put them in your mouth and look at yourself in the mirror. If you can

see nothing, it is well. Test the others in the same way, either in your own mouth, or in that of a child. Those which do not confer invisibility are to be reburied with the head.

TO HAVE GOLD AND SILVER, OR THE HAND OF GLORY

Tear out the hair of a mare in heat, by the roots, closest to the nature, saying DRAGNE, DRAGNE, DRAGNE. Then tie them into a knot. Now go out and buy, without dispute over the price, a new pot of earthenware, which shall have a lid. Return to your house as fast as you can, fill the pot with water from a spring, until it is not quite full. Place the knotted hairs in it, cover it, and place it where neither you nor anyone else can see it, for there is danger in this.

After nine days, at the hidden hour, bring out the pot and open it, and you will find that there is a small animal like a snake therein. This will jump up. Then say: I ACCEPT THE PACT.

Do not touch the animal with your hand. Place it in a new box, which you have bought for this purpose, and that without bargaining as to price. You must feed the creature on wheat-husks alone, daily.

When you need gold or silver, place as much as you require in the box. Go to bed, with the box at the side of the bed. Sleep, if you desire, for three or four hours. Rise, then, and you will find that the money you have placed in the box has been doubled. But what you put first into the box must be left in it.

If it is an ordinary-looking snake, you should not ask for more than one hundred francs at each time. If, however, it has a human face, then you will be able to obtain a thousand francs each time.

If you want to kill the creature, place in the box instead of its daily husks, some of the flour which has been used for the consecration in the first Mass said by the priest. After eating this it will die. Above all, do not omit anything, because this is not intended as a joke!

GARTERS FOR DISTANCES

Go out of the house, fasting; march to your left until you find a ribbon-seller. Buy one ell of white ribbon. Pay what is asked and drop a farthing (un liard) into the box.

Return home by the same route. Next day do the same, until you have found a seller of pens. Buy one, as you bought the ribbon. When you are locked in your own room, write with your own blood on the ribbon the characters of the third line on the plan. This is the right garter. Those of the fourth line are for the left. [It is unknown what these characters are.]

When this is done, go out. The third day after, take your ribbon and pen, walk to the left until you find a pastry cook or bakery. Buy a cake or bread for a halfpenny. Go to the first tavern, order a half bottle of wine, have your glass rinsed three times by the same person, break in three the cake or bread.

Put the three pieces in the glass with wine. Take the first piece and throw it under the table without looking at it, saying IRLY, FOR THEE.

Then take the second piece and throw it likewise, saying TERLY, FOR THEE. Write on the other side of the garter the two names of these spirits with your blood. Throw down the third piece, saying, ERLY, FOR THEE. Throw down the pen, drink the wine without

eating, pay the cost and go away.

Being outside the town, take the garters, make no mistake as to which is the right and which the left. This is important. Stamp three times with the foot on the ground, pronounce the names of the spirits TERLY, ERLY, BALTAZARD, IRLY, MELCHIOR, GASPARD, LET US GO. Then make your trip.

TO MAKE A GIRL DANCE IN THE NUDE

Write on virgin parchment the Character of FRUTIMIERE with the blood of a bat. Then put it on a blessed stone, over which a Mass has been said. After this when you want to use it, place the character under the sill or threshold of a door which she must pass.

When she comes past, she will come in. She will undress and be completely naked, and will dance increasingly until death, if one does not remove the character; with grimaces and contortions which will cause more pity than desire.

TO SEE IN A VISION ANYTHING FROM THE PAST OR FUTURE

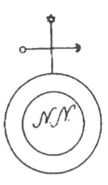

The two N N which you see in the second small circle mark the place where you put your name [see To Make a Girl Come to You...]. To know what you will, write the names in the circle on virgin parchment, before sleeping, and put it under your right ear on retiring, saying the following orison:

Orison

O Glorious Name of Great God the ever-living, to whom all things are present, I am Thy servant N.... Father Eternal, I beg You to send me Thy Holy Angels, who are written in the Circle and that they shall show me what I want to know, by Jesus Christ our Lord. So be it

Having completed the orison, lie down on your right side, and you will see in a dream that which you desire to know.

TO NAIL (AN ENEMY)

Go to a cemetery, remove a nail from an old coffin, saying:

Nails, I take you, so that you may serve to turn aside and cause evil to all persons whom I will. In the Name of the Father, and of the Son, and of the Holy Spirit. Amen..

When you wish to use it, you must look for a footprint and making the three figures of GULAND, SURGAT and MORAIL, fix the nail in the middle saying:

"Pater noster" up to "in terra" [Note: This is the Lord's prayer, in Latin, up to, our father who art on earth]

Hit the nail with a stone, saying:

Curse evil to N . . ., until I remove thee.

Re-cover the place with a little dust, and remember it well, because one cannot remove the evil which this causes, but by removing the nail, and saying:

I remove thee, so that the evil which thou has caused to N..., shall cease. In the Name of the Father, and of the Son. and the Holy Spirit. Amen.

Then take the nail out and efface the characters: not with the same hand as you make them, but with the other. Thus, it will be without danger. [*Note: the sigils of Guland, Surgat, and Morail, are shown in the following list of 44 demons, at their respective listings.*]

FIN

The List of the 44 Demons of the True Grimoire

1. SCIRLIN

This Invocation is to be made on virgin parchment, with the characters of the Demon (you wish to call) upon it, which causes the intermediary Scirlin to come. For from this depend all the others, and it (Scirlin) can constrain them to appear in spite of themselves, as he has the power of Emperor. - *The True Grimoire*

Note: This sigil, as well as those of the eight spirits missing sigils given later in the text, was created by me through the process of "automatic writing" or channeling after invoking the spirit. The sigil represents the magician or witch, symbolized by the circle on the left. The circle on the opposite side represents the spirit one wishes to call, and the lines in between them are the paths taken first by Scirlin to find the spirit, and then by the spirit itself as it comes to you. You can use these sigils in your work with the spirits, or you may channel your own after contacting them.

2. LUCIFER

Lucifer appears in the form and figure of a fair boy. When angry, he seems red. There is nothing monstrous about him. Lucifer has two demons under him: Satanackia and Agalierap. - *The True Grimoire*

Lucifer, the name of the spirit that presides over the orient, according to the opinion of magicians. Lucifer was evoked on Monday, in a circle in the middle of which was his name. He was content with a mouse as the price for his compliance. He is often taken for the king of the underworld, and according to some demonologists, he is superior to Satan. It is said that he is sometimes facetious, and that one of his tricks is to remove the brooms on which the witches go to the Sabbath and to give them rides on his shoulders. This is what the Witches of Moira in Sweden attested in 1672. The same witches claimed that, they had seen, on the Sabbath, this same Lucifer in gray garb, with blue stockings and red pants adorned with ribbons. Lucifer commands the Europeans and Asians. He appears in the form and figure of the most beautiful child. When he is angry, he has a fiery face, but it is nothing monstrous. He is, according to some démonographers, the great vigilante of hell. He is invoked first in the litany of the Sabbath. (*The Dictionnaire Infernal*, 1863)

Notes: Three sigils of Lucifer from the *Grimorium Verum*, illustration from the *Dictionnaire Infernal*, the suit has been added for modern times. The *Grimoire of Honorius* says that he should be invoked on a Monday, and a mouse should be offered to him.

3. SATANACHIA

Under Satanachia or Sataniciae are forty-five, or, according to other versions, fifty-four, daemons. Four of these, the chiefs, are Sergutthy, Heramael, Trimasael and Sustugriel. The others are of no great consequence. - *Grimorium Verum*

Satanachia. He has power over women and girls. He also has the power to make a person young or old. - *The Grand Grimoire*

Notes: Sigil and text from *The Grand Grimoire*; Illustration of Satanchia (next page) created for this book by Ville Vuorinen.

(*Satanchia*, by Ville Vuorinen)

4. SERGUTTHY

Sergutthy has power over maidens and wives, when things are favorable. - *Grimorium Verum*

5. HERAMAEL

Heramael teaches the art of healing, including the complete knowledge of any illness and its cure, He also makes known the virtues of plants, where they are to be found, when to pluck them, and their making into a complete cure. - *The True Grimoire*

6. TRIMASAEL

Trimasael teaches chemistry and all means of conjuring of the nature of deceit or sleight-of-hand. He also teaches the secret of making the Powder of Projection, by means of which the base metals may be turned into gold or silver. - *The True Grimoire*

7. SUSTUGRIEL

Sustugriel teaches the art of magic. He gives familiar spirits that can be used for all purposes, and he also gives mandragores.

- *Grimorium Verum*

8. AGALIEREPT

Agalierept and Tarchimache (Lucifuge Rofocale) are the rulers of Elelogap, who in turn governs matters connected with water.
- *Grimorium Verum*

Agaliarept, who has the power to discover the most hidden secrets, in all the Courts and Governments of the world, he reveals the greatest mysteries. He commands the second legion of spirits, he has under him Buer, Gusoan and Botis. - *The Grand Grimoire*

Notes: Sigil from *The Grand Grimoire*; illustration of Agaliarept (opposite page) created for this book by Artem Grigoryev.

9. ELELOGAP

Agalierept and Tarchimache (Lucifuge Rofocale) are the rulers of Elelogap, who in turn governs matters connected with water.

- *The True Grimoire.*

Notes: We have very little to go on concerning the nature of this spirit. My feeling on this one is that it is something similar to a fish god like Dagon. I created this sigil after invoking the spirit. The sigil symbolizes a half man/half fish god, rising from the waves.

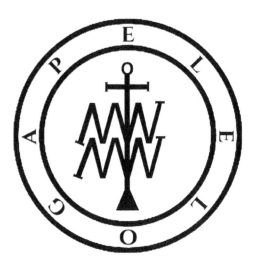

10. BEELZEBUTH

Beelzebuth appears sometimes in monstrous forms, sometimes like a giant cow, at times like a he-goat, with a long tail. When angry, he vomits fire. - *Grimorium Verum*

Beelzebub or Belzebub or Beelzebuth. Prince of Demons, according to the scriptures; The first in power and in crime after Satan. According to Milton: Supreme leader of the Infernal Empire, according to most démonographers. – His name means *Lord of the Flies*. Bodin claims that he is no longer seen in his temple. It was the Demon most revered of the peoples of Canaan, who sometimes represented him under the figure of a fly, most often with the attributes of the sovereign power. He made Oracles, and King Ochozias consulted him on a sickness which worried him and was severely reprimanded for this by the prophet Elisha. He was given the power to deliver the men from the flies that ruined the harvest. Almost all the démonomanes look at him as the ruler of the Dark Empire, and each one portrays him according to his imagination.

Milton gives him an imposing appearance, and a high wisdom breathes on his face. Some says he is as high as a tower; others, of a size equal to ours. Some of them describe him in the form of a snake with the traits of a woman. The monarch of the underworld, says Palingène, in Zodiaco Vitœ, is of a prodigious size, seated on an immense throne, surrounded by a ring of fire, swollen chest, puffy face, gleaming eyes, raised eyebrows and menacing air. It has extremely wide nostrils, and two large horns on the head; He is black as a moor: two broad wings of bats are attached to his shoulders; It has two broad duck legs, a lion's tail, and long hairs from the head to the feet. Some say that Beelzebub is Priapus; Others, like Porphyry, confuse him with Bacchus. It was thought to be found in the Belbog or Belbach (white God) of the Slavons, because his bloody image was always covered with flies, like that of Beelzebub among the Syrians. It is also said to be the same as Pluto. (*The Dictionnaire Infernal*)

Notes: Illustration from *The Dictionnaire Infernal*; sigils from *The True Grimoire,* and *The Grand Grimoire*.

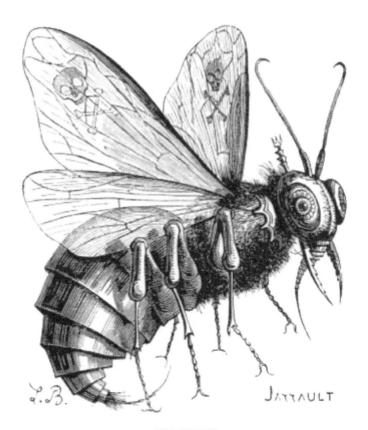

BELZEBUB

11. LUCIFUGE ROFOCALE

The first (of the subordinate spirits in the order of *The Grand Grimoire*) is the great Lucifuge Rofocale, the infernal Prime Minister who possesses the power that Lucifer gave him over all worldly riches and treasures. He has beneath him Bael, Agares and Marbas along with thousands of other demons or spirits who are his subordinates. - *The Grand Grimoire*.

Notes: Illustration and sigil from *The Grand Grimoire*.

12. FLEURETY

The fourth of the subordinate spirits in the order of *The Grand Grimoire* is the Lieutenant General Fleurety, who has the power to perform any task he wishes during the night. He can also cause hail or raise a storm where he wishes. He commands a very considerable corps of spirits, and he has under him Bathim, Parsan and Abigar. - *The Grand Grimoire*.

Notes: Sigil from *The Grand Grimoire*; Illustration of Fleurety (next page) by Matti Sinkkonen.

(*Fleurety*, by Matti Sinkkonen)

13. ASTAROTH

Astaroth appears black, in human shape - *The Grimorium Verum*

Astaroth great-Mighty Duke in the underworld. He has the figure of a very ugly angel and shows himself straddling an infernal
dragon; He holds in his left hand a viper. Some magicians say that
he presides over the West, that he provides the friendship of the
Great Lords, and that he must be evoked on Wednesday. The

Sidonians and the Philistines adored him. (as the goddess Astarte) He is said to be the great treasurer in Hell. Wierus teaches us that he knows the past and the future, and that he would be happy to answer questions that we ask to him on the most secret things. It is easy to cause him to talk about the creation and, the faults and the fall of the Angels, about which he knows the whole story. But in his conversations, he argues that for him he was punished unjustly. He teaches liberal arts in depth, and commands forty legions. He who invokes this spirit must be careful to let himself be approached, because of his unbearable stench. That is why it is prudent for the magician to hold under his nostrils a magic ring, made of silver, which is a protection against the evil odors of demons. Astaroth has been present in several possessions. He is quoted as one of the seven princes of hell who visited Faust, according to the English tradition. He appeared as a snake with a colorful tail like changing bricks, two short feet, all yellow, white and yellowish belly, reddish brown neck, and arrow points, like those of the hedgehog, as long as the length of a finger. (*The Dictionnaire Infernal*)

(29.) Astaroth - The Twenty-ninth Spirit is Astaroth. He is a Mighty, Strong Duke, and appeareth in the Form of an hurtful Angel riding on an Infernal Beast like a Dragon, and carrying in his right hand a Viper. Thou must in no wise let him approach too near unto thee, lest he do thee damage by his Noisome Breath. Wherefore the Magician must hold the Magical Ring near his face, and that will defend him. He giveth true answers of things Past, Present, and to Come, and can discover all Secrets. He will declare wittingly how the Spirits fell, if desired, and the reason of his own fall. He can make men wonderfully knowing in all Liberal Sciences. He ruleth 40 Legions of Spirits.

His Seal is this, which wear thou as a Lamen before thee, or else he will not appear nor yet obey thee, etc. - *The Lesser Key of Solomon*

Notes: Illustration from *The Dictionnaire Infernal*; sigils from *The True Grimoire* and *The Grand Grimoire*. *The Grimoire of Honorius* says that he is to be invoked on a Wednesday, and that a little bread must be given him. It also says that he makes men happy and discovers treasures.

ASTAROTH

14. SARGATANAS

The fifth (of the subordinate spirits listed in *The Grand Grimoire*) is Brigadier Sargatanas, who has the power to make one invisible, to transport one anywhere, to open all locks, to grant one the power to see whatever is happening inside homes, to teach all the tricks and subtleties of the Shepherds. He controls several brigades of spirits. He has under him Loray, Valefar and Farau. - *The Grand Grimoire*

Notes: Sigil from *The Grand Grimoire*; Illustration of Sargatanas (opposite page) created for this book by Ville Vuorinen.

15. NEBIROS

The sixth Superior Spirit (of the list in *The Grand Grimoire*) is Nebiros, Camp Marshal and Inspector General, who has the power to harm whoever he pleases, he can reveal the Hand of Glory, he educates on all the qualities of Metals, Minerals, Plants and all pure & impure Animals. He also grants the art of predicting the future, being one of the greatest necromancers of all the infernal spirits. He can go anywhere and inspect all the infernal militias. He has under him Ayperos, Nuberus and Glasyabolas. - *The Grand Grimoire*

Notes: Sigil from *The Grand Grimoire*; illustration of Nebiros (opposite page) created for this book by Ville Vuorinen.

16. HAEL

Hael enables anyone to speak in any language he wishes, and also, he teaches the means whereby any type of letter may be written. He is also able to teach those things which are most secret and completely hidden. - *The True Grimoire*

17. SERGULATH

Sergulath gives every means of speculation. In addition, he instructs as to the methods of breaking the ranks and strategy of opponents. - *The True Grimoire.*

18. PROCULO

Proculo, who can cause a person to sleep for forty-eight hours, with the knowledge of the spheres of sleep. - *Grimorium Verum*

Notes: This sigil was created by me and represents a soul (the circle at the top) coming loose from the body (represented by the cross-like figure at the bottom) thus, to wander in the dream world.

19. HARISTUM

Haristum, who can cause anyone to pass through fire without being touched by it. - *Grimorium Verum*

Notes: Sigil created by me and represents the motion of a human (the circle), the line with the arrow, passing through flames.

20. BRULEFER

Brulefer, who causes a person to be beloved of women. - *The True Grimoire*

Notes: This sigil was created by me, and it represents masculine energy (the points) reaching for the feminine (the circles).

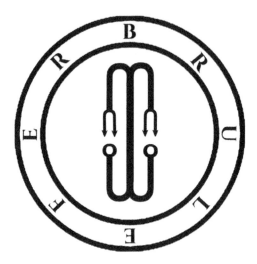

21. PENTAGNONY

Pentagnony, who gives the two benefits of attaining invisibility and the love of great lords. - *The Grimorium Verum*

Notes: Sigil created by the author, the union of the symbol of Saturn, invisibility, and Jupiter, the love of great lords.

22. AGLASIS

Aglasis, who can carry anyone or anything anywhere in the world.

- Grimorium Verum

Notes: Sigil created by the author, the middle bar represents the line between "here" and "there." The arrows represent travel to "there" and back again. Illustration (opposite page) created for this book by Artem Grigoryev.

23. SIDRAGOSAM

Sidragosam, causes any girl to dance in the nude. - *The True Grimoire*
Notes: Sigil created by the author, the large "T" represents the
demon Sidragosam, and the smaller "T" represents the dancing girl.
Illustration (opposite page) created for this book by Ville Vuorinen.

24. MINOSON

Minoson, is able to make anyone win at any game. - *Grimorium Verum*

Notes: Sigil created by the author, represents the emotional feeling of winning.

25. BUCON

Bucon, can cause hate and spiteful jealousy between members of the opposite sexes. - *The True Grimoire.*

Notes: Sigil created by the author, the circle with the dot in the center represents the "eye of the mind" releasing the point, and the waves, and the smaller dots, which are meant to give the general feel of the mind experiencing jealousy.

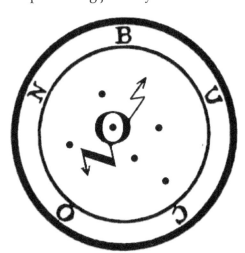

26. SYRACH

There are yet other daemons, apart from these, who are under Duke Syrach. There are eighteen of these, and their names are:

I. Clauneck	X. Segal
II. Musisin	XI. Hicpacth
III. Bechaud	XII. Humots
IV. Frimost	XIII. Frucissiere
V. Klepoth	XIV. Guland
VI. Khil	XV. Surgat
VII. Mersilde	XVI. Morail
VIII. Clisthert	XVII. Frutimiere
IX. Sirchade	XVIII. Huictiigaras

Notes: All we know of Duke Syrach is that he is a mighty General who commands the 18 mighty spirits under him. Sigil from the *Secrets of Solomon*.

27. CLAUNECK

Clauneck has power over riches, can cause treasures to be found. He can give great riches to he who makes a pact with him, for he is much loved by Lucifer. It is he who causes money to be brought.
- *Grimorium Verum*

Notes: Sigils from the *Secrets of Solomon* and *The True Grimoire*. Illustration of Clauneck from the 1863 *Dictionnaire Infernal*.

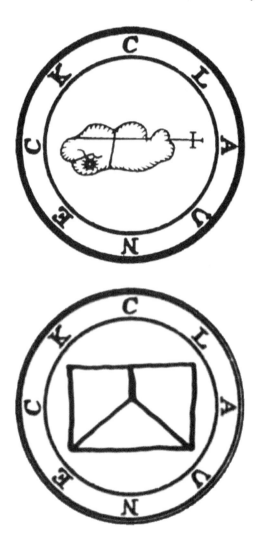

28. MUSISIN

Musisin has power over great lords, teaches all that happens in the Republics, and the affairs of the Allies. - *Grimorium Verum*

Notes: Sigils from *The True Grimoire* and the *Secrets of Solomon*.

29. BECHARD

Bechard is a demon described in the *Keys of Solomon* as having power over winds and storms. He causes hail, storms and rain, by means of a malefic curse that he composes with stewed toads and other drugs. - *Dictionnaire Infernal* (Translated from the French by Aaman Lamba.)

Notes: Text from *The Dictionnaire Infernal*; Sigil from *The Grimorium Verum*. The illustration of a toad represents Bechard. *The grimoire of Honorius* says that he should be invoked on a Friday and given a nut.

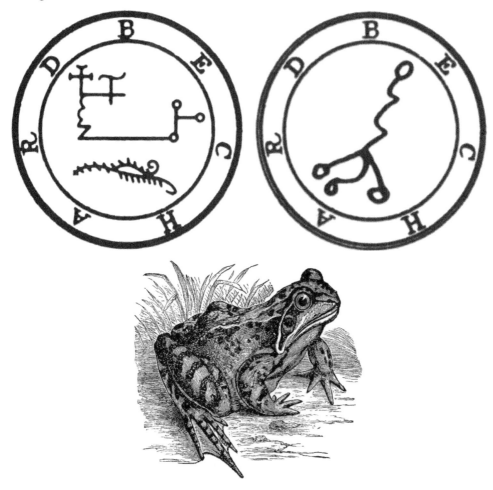

30. FRIMOST

Frimost has power over women and girls and will help you to obtain their use. - *The True Grimoire*

Notes: Sigils from *The Grimorium Verum* and the *Secrets of Solomon*. *The Grimoire of Honorius* says that he should be invoked on a Tuesday, the first stone one finds should be given him, and that he is to be treated with dignity and honor. He is also called Nambroth in *The Grimoire of Honorius*.

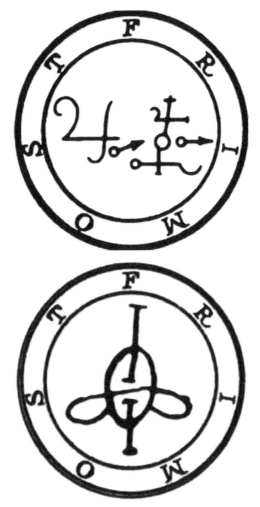

31. KLEPOTH

Klepoth makes you see all sorts of dreams and visions. - *The True Grimoire*

Notes: Sigils from *The Grimorium Verum* and the *Secrets of Solomon*.

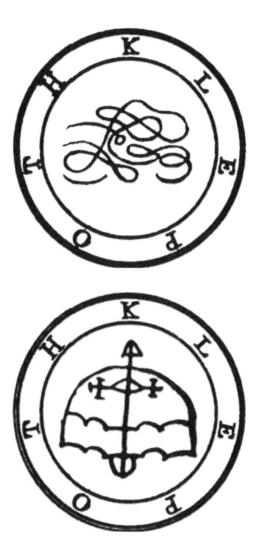

32. KHIL

Khil makes great earthquakes. - *The True Grimoire*

Notes: Sigil from *The Grimorium Verum*

33. MERSILDE

Mersilde has the power to transport anyone in an instant, any-where. - *The True Grimoire*

34. CLISTHERT

Clisthert allows you to have day or night, whichever you wish, when you desire either. - *Grimorium Verum*

Notes: Sigil from *The Grimorium Verum*

35. SIRCHADE

Sirchade makes you see all sorts of natural and supernatural animals. - *The Grimorium Verum*

Notes: *The Grimoire of Honorius* says that Sirchade is attributed to Thursday.

36. SEGAL

Segal will cause all sorts of prodigies to appear. - *The True Grimoire*

37. HICPACTH

Hicpacth will bring you a person in an instant, though he be far away. - *Grimorium Verum*

38. HUMOTS

Humots can bring you any book you desire. - *The True Grimoire*

Notes: Illustration (next page) created for this book by Jenny Kelevra.

(*Humots*, by Jenny Kelevra)

39. FRUCISSIERE

Frucissiere revives the dead. - *The Grimorium Verum*

Notes: Illustration of Frucissiere (next page) created for this book by Ville Vuorinen.

(*Frucissiere*, by Ville Vuorinen)

40. GULAND

Guland causes all illnesses. - *The True Grimoire*

Notes: *The Grimoire of Honorius* says that he should be invoked on a Saturday and offered burned bread.

41. SURGAT

Surgat opens every kind of lock. - *Grimorium Verum*

Notes: *The Grimoire of Honorius* says that he should be invoked on a Sunday, and offered the hair of a fox, even though he demands a hair of your head. It also states that his office is to discover and transport all treasures, and perform anything that you wish.

42. MORAIL

Morail can make anything invisible. - *Grimorium Verum*

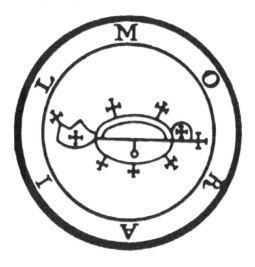

43. FRUTIMIERE

Frutimiere prepares all kinds of feasts for you. - *The True Grimoire*

44. HUICTIIGARAS

Huictiigaras causes sleep in the case of some, and insomnia in others. - *Grimorium Verum*

Final Thoughts

This book is dedicated to all of the people who have helped me become an author; to the artists Ville Vuorinen, Matti Sinkkonen, Artem Grigoryev, and Jenny Kelevra; and also to the graphic designers and editors who have helped transform my vision into reality: Gregory K. Koon, David Rankine, and Jeysin Wahrheit; and to the demon of books, Humots, who came through in so many ways to make my books a reality.

And finally to you, dear reader. May you discover true magic and walk in its ways forever.

Printed in Great Britain
by Amazon

41527298R00078